Colors of Hope

Painting on a Canvas of Pain with Colors of Hope

Shawn Wood

To the God of miracles,

You did it again.

To Connie,

In my hopeless days you have always been hope to me.
You are what God knew I needed.

To Freedom Church,

Your support of this dream that became the movement called
Freedom Church is one of the most audacious decisions I
have ever seen a group of people make.
Let's keep offering hope to people in their pain and seeing
God do His miracles.

CONTENTS

WELCOME

Note from the Author

Thank you for picking up *Colors of Hope*! As you read, you'll notice that a workbook section, including reflective questions and application-oriented "action steps," follows each main chapter of the book. These questions and action steps are intended to help you move past your current problems, worries, and pain by seeking God in faith—believing He has an incredible story of hope ready to be painted on your canvas of pain.

The workbook sections can be used for independent reflection, discussion with a friend, or group study. You can use the spaces provided to write down your responses, and each chapter concludes with a page to record your thoughts and other notes as well.

No matter your reason for picking up this book, my prayer is that reading it will help you strengthen your faith and grow closer to the God of miracles.

—Shawn Wood

4 · SHAWN WOOD

Leaving with a Miracle

Have you ever witnessed a miracle? Merriam-Webster defines a miracle as "an extraordinary event manifesting divine intervention in human affairs."[1] A miracle, then, is something both *divine* and *extraordinary*, a moment when a person's life intersects with God.

There are 125 recorded miracles in the Bible. Well, at least that's what some sources say.[2] Biblical scholars seem unable to agree on exactly how many miracles are in the Bible. To some extent, that debate may be reflective of the larger problem when it comes to miracles.

While some see miracles, others are so clouded with pain that they can't seem to embrace the elements of wonder and mystery in the Bible. And if we're honest, it's easy to question certain miracles in the Bible:

Did a fish really swallow Jonah and spit him back out to tell the story?

Did Jesus really raise Lazarus from the dead after his body started to decay?

Did Philip the Evangelist actually move from one place to another in a *Star Trek*-like teleport?

Did these miracles really happen, and do these types of things happen today?

Maybe we can agree, at least, that lots of miracles occurred in the Bible. And possibly, by the end of this book, we can also agree that everyone reading this book is one more miracle to add to that list.

Do you believe a miracle could happen to you?

Here is an even more unsettling question: Do you think you could see miracles happen *because* of you? Jesus said, "I tell you the truth, anyone who believes in me will do the same works I have done, and even greater works, because I am going to be with the Father" (John 14:12 NLT). Jesus intended His followers to see and experience miracles. Jesus intended His followers to bring hope and healing to people.

This book will look at the seven miracles of Jesus and how those miracles occurred to people in the midst of loss, disappointment, and discouragement. Their lives were really a blank canvas of pain, waiting for kaleidoscopic colors of hope to illuminate the blank space.

As you read these accounts, ask yourself:

Have I left margin in my life to allow for a divine, extraordinary move of God?

Do I believe not only that these miracles in the past did happen, but that miracles can and will happen in my own life?

Do I recognize a miracle of God when it comes, or do I take credit for what is really God's work?

I bet some of us just may find that we are already a work of God's incredible craftsmanship and have not even realized it. First, consider an Old Testament story to help prepare your heart with what precedes a miracle: *expectancy.*

The Birth of a Miracle

I love the story of the Shunammite woman of 2 Kings 4 because she reminds me of some of the soulful women I grew up around in the low country of South Carolina—plain-spoken, family-oriented, and tough as nails. She had a heart open to God and recognized His direct intervention.

As you read the story you will see that this woman and her husband regularly invited the prophet Elisha to come and eat with them. A relationship grew and eventually this wealthy couple built and furnished a room over the garage—we in the South call that a FROG—so that the man of God could stay with them whenever he was in town.

Their generosity was the first setup for the miracle that would happen in their lives. I wonder how many miracles I have missed in my life simply by not being generous. Maybe God flows things to me so I can be in a place of preparation for a miracle.

One day he came there, and he turned into the chamber and rested there. And he said to Gehazi his servant, "Call this Shunammite." When he had called her, she stood before him. And he said to him, "Say now to her, 'See, you have taken all this trouble for us; what is to be done for you? Would you have a word spoken on your behalf to the king or commander of the army?'" She answered, "I dwell among my own people." And he said, "What then is to be done for her?" Gehazi answered, "Well, she has no son, and her husband is old." He said, "Call her." And when he had called her, she stood in the doorway. And he said, "At this season, about this time next year, you shall embrace a son."— **2 Kings 4:11–16a (ESV)**

I love the Shunammite woman's answer, even though it is probably just a little bit sassy. She said, "I dwell among my own people" (2 Kings 4:13 ESV). In other words, she was telling Elisha, "I am good. I have a husband who takes care of me. I have servants who help me. I am in a good place of acceptance of my life."

Acceptance is something that we long for, isn't it? It's comfortable to come to a place in life where we do not have to dream anymore and can accept that our life is, well, what it is. We rename this "contentment" because if you can put a virtuous- or biblical-sounding word on top of disappointment, it can cover up the ugliness of a life where God's big dreams for us have been buried.

We don't really enjoy expectancy. The opportunity for pain is ample within expectancy. You expect your husband to change and be the man you need, but again, he doesn't. You expect the promotion this time. Again, it does not come. You expect a great health report after the chemo that almost killed you. It does not come. More chemo.

Have you ever been there? A place where the dream you used to have has become so far-fetched that it ceases to be a dream at all?

The man of God, though, does something that every single believer has the capacity to do: he ushers in expectancy. Unmet, unseen expectancy. I like to call it "hope."

God says, "I know what you used to dream about. A son. I know what dream you have let slip out of sight and out of mind. I know what is hidden deep in the linguistic corridors of your simple answer, 'I am fine,' and it is called the hope of a dream." Through the prophet Elisha, God spoke life over the Shunammite women—and acceptance changed to expectancy.

Dreams Buried in Discouragement

The thought of God working a miracle in your life may be exciting, but it can also bring up the pain of past hurts and failures. When the Shunammite woman heard this great promise from God, her response was not elation and gratitude as one might expect.

Instead, she said, perhaps a bit perplexed, "No, my lord, O man of God; do not lie to your servant" (2 Kings 4:16b ESV).

When God wants to birth a miracle inside of you, often the pain and fear of revisiting hopes and dreams that you have buried may prevent you from fully embracing God's work in your life. Your first reaction might be, "Don't get my hopes up again," or "Let's just leave that dream buried," or "It's probably better this way." Likely this is what happened with the Shunammite woman—her dream for a son had probably been almost forgotten. But that little flicker of hope is more than just emotion; it's actually expectancy.

Sometimes a dream is buried so deep in hurt and discouragement it takes someone else to call it out. Elisha recognized the Shunammite woman's dream and confidently told her, "At this season, about this time next year, you shall embrace a son" (2 Kings 4:16 ESV). The woman had little faith for this miracle, but Elisha had faith for the two of them. Scripture says the following spring the woman became pregnant and bore a son "as Elisha had said to her" (2 Kings 4:17 ESV).

There may be someone you know who has given up on God's miracle in their life. Perhaps God wants you to be an Elisha to them—to believe better things about them than they believe about themselves, to speak life to them, and to share with them a fresh word from God.

So God blessed the Shunammite woman and her husband with a son, even though her husband was old—but it began with a dream, with expectancy. The woman longed for a son.

God wants not merely to change your circumstances, but to give birth to a miracle inside of you—something bigger than you could accomplish on your own, something where the numbers and statistics don't make sense. As closed as you may be to your heart's desire, God cuts right through your soul to your point of need.

Maybe God wants you to start—or continue—a vocation, a ministry, or a movement that will bring glory to Him. Maybe your miracle will be to revive something that is almost gone. Perhaps God is calling you to begin a new partnership or to strengthen a faltering relationship. Maybe the miracle would be the restoration of a relationship that seems absolutely dead and hopeless.

God may have a physical miracle for you, as He did for the Shunammite woman. Or it may be something more profound. One of the most profound but easily overlooked miracles is a changed heart and life.

When the Miracle Dies

Sometimes God will allow a miracle to die and it doesn't make sense. Perhaps you had been obedient and had been walking in God's favor. Doors had opened. You experienced abundance and sensed God's blessing, and then, without warning, everything became painfully difficult or even hopeless. Your business went under. Your hope of having a family was shattered. Or your dream for your family was destroyed.

This is what happened to the Shunammite woman. One day, unexpectedly, something tragic occurred:

> When the child had grown, he went out one day to his father among the reapers. And he said to his father, "Oh, my head, my head!" The father said to his servant, "Carry him to his mother." And when he had lifted him and brought him to his mother, the child sat on her lap till noon, and then he died. And she went up and laid him on the bed of the man of God and shut the door behind him and went out. — **2 Kings 4:18–21 (ESV)**

A person's natural first thought in these situations is often, "Where are you, God?" The Shunammite woman was no different. But rather than give in to despair, she clung to faith in God's promises. Something amazing happens when God starts to paint with colors of hope on the canvas of your life. These pictures of hope are so bright a reminder that they will encourage you for seasons to come.

God had brought the Shunammite woman this child. She had learned from God's past work in her life that she could be expectant about what He would do in the future, even though the present situation looked bleak.

It's Gonna Be All Right

The son—the dream the Shunammite woman longed for had died. One would expect a mother to slide into a deep depression, but the Shunammite woman's response was quite different:

> Then she called to her husband and said, "Send me one of the servants and one of the donkeys, that I may quickly go to the man of God and come back again." And he said, "Why will you go to him today? It is neither new moon nor Sabbath." She said, "All is well." — **2 Kings 4:22–23 (ESV)**

All is well? Her son was dead! She didn't tell her husband the story, but instead said, "It's gonna be all right." This was not fake religiosity that everything was great when it wasn't. Sometimes the most margin a person can leave for a miracle is enough faith to doubt. God had miraculously given her a son, and this woman had enough faith to doubt her son was really dead. Her actions next reflected her faith:

Then she saddled the donkey, and she said to her servant, "Urge the animal on; do not slacken the pace for me unless I tell you." So she set out and came to the man of God at Mount Carmel. When the man of God saw her coming, he said to Gehazi his servant, "Look, there is the Shunammite. Run at once to meet her and say to her, 'Is all well with you? Is all well with your husband? Is all well with the child?' And she answered, "All is well." And when she came to the mountain to the man of God, she caught hold of his feet. And Gehazi came to push her away. But the man of God said, "Leave her alone, for she is in bitter distress, and the LORD has hidden it from me and has not told me." Then she said, "Did I ask my lord for a son? Did I not say, 'Do not deceive me?'" — **2 Kings 4:24–28 (ESV)**

She was expectant, but she was also honest with her feelings—she had come to accept her fate of childlessness. Elisha was the one who sought God to fulfill her dream to bear a son.

She angrily charged Elisha with playing with her emotions, saying in effect, "Did I ask you for this dream? No! I was fine with just going through the motions and pretending everything was fine. You gave this miracle to me, so now why are you playing with me?"

Ultimately, the woman was questioning God. Perhaps she thought, *You started this work of art on my soul God—you can finish it.*

Sometimes when a person's miracle dies, they stop listening to God's Word. They stop going to church and stop putting themselves in places where God speaks most clearly. "It didn't do any good," they believe.

This was not the Shunammite woman's response, however. She presented hard questions, but she ran as fast as she could *to* God before she lost faith. She took her questions directly to the man of God, Elisha, rather than letting them distance her from God. She didn't settle for pat answers, but showed a tenacity and determination in the face of all her doubts.

Elisha's response may have seemed odd. He first commanded Gehazi to lay Elisha's staff on the boy's face:

> Tie up your garment and take my staff in your hand and go. If you meet anyone, do not greet him, and if anyone greets you, do not reply. And lay my staff on the face of the child. — **2 Kings 4:29 (ESV)**

The boy's mother's response reflected her faith—she would not be left behind. "As the LORD lives and as you yourself live, I will not leave you," she firmly declared (2 King 4:30 ESV). I love this mama-bear level of determination. Elisha knew in no uncertain terms what she expected, and it was nothing short of a miracle.

Gehazi arrived on the scene first and laid the staff on the dead child's face, "but there was no sound or sign of life" (2 Kings 4:31 ESV). So, Gehazi returned to Elisha and announced, "The child has not awakened" (2 Kings 4:31 ESV).

No miracle occurred.

Just Try Some Stuff

Apparently, Elisha's staff had been the tool God had used in the past. This time, however, nothing happened. The boy was still dead. But just because Elisha's first attempt at a resurrection didn't work didn't mean it was time to quit.

Elisha knew the woman was waiting for him if he failed. So, he tried a different approach:

> When Elisha came into the house, he saw the child lying dead on his bed. So he went in and shut the door behind the two of them and prayed to the LORD. Then he went up and lay on the child, putting his mouth on his mouth, his eyes on his eyes, and his hands on his hands. And as he stretched himself upon him, the flesh of the child became warm. — **2 Kings 4:32–34**

There are times when following Jesus means pressing on alone. It may mean metaphorically shutting the door to block the voices that say, "It's time to quit and move on." Now, there is a time for moving on—you will know when. It's usually not as quick as one would like. But most of the time, it is not time to quit. We just need to get alone with God and try to hear from Him. When what has worked in the past doesn't work anymore, don't stop trying—attempt something different.

I remember one of the most freeing moments for me was a conversation with my friend Pastor Steven Furtick just before we started Freedom Church. He said, "The most I am ever sure God is speaking to me is about eighty percent." In other words, don't wait until you have every detail before you move forward.

Step out and try what you believe God is directing you to do, even if you can't see how things will work out. You will miss the miracle if you wait for God to tell you everything. If you wait for the other twenty percent to become clear or for the perfect time, you'll be waiting forever. Step out in faith and try, even if you have no idea what to do.

There is something easy to miss in this story, but I think it's critically important: it's a strange miracle. A child is dead, and his mother irate. A preacher spreads himself over the dead child. Come on, don't act so holy— admit that this is weird!

However, I am finding in life that God's path to a miracle will take you places you've never been and are probably uncomfortable going. In Elisha's case, he "lay on the child, putting his mouth on his mouth, his eyes on his eyes, and his hands on his hands" (2 Kings 4:34). Elisha's experience is one small example of what can happen when we believe God for a miracle:

> Then he got up again and walked once back and forth in the house, and went up and stretched himself upon him. The child sneezed seven times, and the child opened his eyes. Then he summoned Gehazi and said, "Call this Shunammite." So he called her. And when she came to him, he said, "Pick up your son." She came and fell at his feet, bowing to the ground. Then she picked up her son and went out. — **2 Kings 4:35–37 (ESV)**

Though there were some strange responses— including seven sneezes—the boy comes alive. God is a divine and extraordinary God. Nothing is impossible with Him! (Matthew 19:26). If nothing is impossible, anything can happen.

You may come into the presence of God with a dead dream, like the Shunammite woman, but you will leave with a divine miracle.

Will you join me in examining seven of Jesus' miracles, and the lives and faith of the people those miracles affected?

CHAPTER ONE

Inviting a Miracle

People tend to desire the supernatural as proof, don't we? We see miracles, signs, and wonders as something we can use to prove God's existence. It is our get-out-of-faith card, if you will, and it seems to be true for those who follow Jesus as well as for those who don't.

When someone is sick or dying, people—even those who do not follow Jesus—typically pray for healing. As a pastor, I have had many people tell me over hospital visits that they have prayed that God would prove Himself to them through their healing or the healing of a loved one.

When there is a problem, it is human nature to pray for a solution.

I don't think this disappoints God. Rather, I think He kind of enjoys proving Himself. However, God's economy is so much grander. Though He desires those things, too, His purposes are beyond the sign or miracle being prayed for. The Christ-follower's job is not to pray for miracles, but to let God birth a miracle inside them that they might *be* the miracles of God.

The very first recorded miracle of Jesus took place at a wedding in Cana. This is how New Testament scholar Leon Morris describes the wedding traditions of the time:

According to the Mishnah [Jewish oral law, as opposed to the written Torah] the wedding would take place on a Wednesday if the bride was a virgin and on a Thursday if she was a widow (Ket. 1:1). The bridegroom and his friends made their way in procession to the bride' s house. This was often done at night, when there could be a spectacular torchlight procession. There were doubtless speeches and expressions of goodwill before the bride and groom went in procession to the groom' s house, where the wedding banquet was held. It is probable that there was a religious ceremony, but we have no details. The processions and the feast are the principal items of which we have knowledge. The feast was prolonged, and might last as long as a week.[3]

The apostle John wrote of this wedding in Cana:

On the third day a wedding took place at Cana in Galilee. Jesus' mother was there, and Jesus and his disciples had also been invited to the wedding.
— **John 2:1–2 (NIV)**

It wasn't by chance Jesus' first miracle happened at this wedding. It occurred "on the third day," only three days after Jesus had called His first disciples (John 1:35–50), who had also been invited to attend. Jesus' disciples were about to witness something unexplainable.

Invite Jesus to the Party

The first step to this miracle was that the couple invited Jesus to their wedding. I can't guarantee specific miracles will occur when following Jesus, but I can guarantee an *absence* of miracles if Jesus is not invited into a person's life!

I also love the relational lesson in this story of Jesus. Though Jesus is God and was always purposefully "on mission" on earth, He did not hesitate to attend a simple wedding in Cana because He loved people. He cared about the details in their lives. He came to earth to be with and save people.

As people who follow Jesus, we should in turn model this. To be a part of God's miracle in someone's life, we need to step out and engage with and love people, as Jesus did. We need to be a part of the everyday as well as the extra-special happenings in people's lives.

Sometimes I am guilty of seeing the relational side of a miracle-inducing life as a hindrance—and maybe even seeing people as a hindrance. Jesus did not. He saw people as the miracle.

Pursue the Miracle

Mary, Jesus' mother, was a guest at the wedding, although her role seems to have been more than that of a guest. Scripture implies the couple being married were either Mary's close friends or possibly related to her. Mary was helping with the arrangements, especially serving the food and wine. She seemed to have been one of the first to realize the wine was running out, which would have brought shame to the host family.

In fact, as I write this, I am confident Mary may have been that aunt every wedding has as the wedding coordinator, whose job is to ensure the groomsmen don't act like fools, everyone is in the right order, and the flower girl and ring bearer make it down the aisle. I have run into a few such women in my years as a pastor, and one can only hope that Jesus' mother was not nearly as ornery as one of these wedding-coordinating aunts!

> When the wine was gone, Jesus' mother said to him, "They have no more wine."
>
> "Woman, why do you involve me?" Jesus replied. "My hour has not yet come." His mother said to the servants, "Do whatever He tells you." — **John 2:3–5 (NIV)**

Now, everyone knows how Mary delivered this message, because we all have moms. It was with slightly gritted teeth, an intense whisper, as if to say, "Keep this to yourself," combined with the implication that "I am your mother and you had better do something about this."

Jesus' initial response indicated the shortage of wine was not His problem. Some have said that Mary was anxious for Him to reveal Himself as the Messiah. Honestly, I am not sure that was her intent. I think she had a need in her life, and the natural response of those who have encountered Jesus is to run to Him with their needs.

And ultimately, does it really matter why we need a miracle at the point of desperation in our lives?

Mary's faith, or her desire not to be embarrassed, moved her to tell the servants to do whatever Jesus told them to do. She knew Jesus was able to solve the problem, but trusted He would do so on His own accord.

What if we decided to do whatever Jesus told us to do? What if we purposed that whatever we read in the Bible, we would obey?

Unfortunately, my attitude (and I bet yours as well) often reflects a different response to God: "Whoa, I didn't know all this was going to be required. God, can You just do something without me having to do all that? I want You to work in my life, God, but I can't be *that* available.

I call it the "Meat Loaf" answer to God: "I will do anything for You—but I won't do *that*."

Instead, our attitude should be, "God, my answer is yes! Now what is the question?"

Mary saw the shortage of wine as an opportunity, not a problem. I guess every person has a shortage in some area. Perhaps you are short on faith or hope. Perhaps there is a deficit of love in your life, leaving you feeling unworthy or unwanted. Perhaps you have a financial shortage or a relational shortage.

Your shortage is an empty white space on the canvas of your life, waiting for what God wants to paint on your life.

Many biblical miracles began with a person's own initiative, not God's. The *pursuit* of a miracle opens the *pathway* to a miracle. Jesus told Mary He was not seeking to perform a miracle at the wedding. Nonetheless, Mary pushed a little in faith.

Scripture is full of other examples of people pressing into Jesus in faith. The bleeding woman touched the hem of Jesus' garment when He was on the way to help someone else (Matthew 9:20). Naaman came from another kingdom to ask Elisha for healing from leprosy (2 Kings 5). The centurion sought out Jesus to heal his servant (Luke 7:1–10).

Push against that brick wall until one step opens. Then take that step and push a little bit harder until the next step opens. God doesn't want us to sit back and hope He will do something. Often, Christians spiritualize their passivity by saying, "I'm going to let God be God, and I'm going to stay out of it. He is going to do what He wants to do, anyway."

The only problem with that attitude is the Bible.

The Bible says followers of Jesus should approach Him like the woman with a legal issue who went to the judge's door. The judge told her to go away, but she kept banging on the door. Finally, the judge became so annoyed that he decided to do something (Luke 18:1–8).

Jesus said Christians should have that kind of tenacity with God. They should *pursue* a miracle. They should go before Him and say, "God, this is what I think You want to do in my life. I'm going to step out and ask for it. I'm going to knock on the door. I'm going to trust You to order my steps in the right way."

Many miracles involve God's supernatural intervention, but also a human expectation that leads to an obedient action. The Israelites had to walk through the Red Sea after God parted it (Exodus 14). Joshua and his army had to march around the walls of Jericho before it fell (Joshua 6:3–20). The blind man had to wash the mud off his eyes in the pool of Siloam (John 9:7). When it comes to miracles you want to see in and through your life, God expects your obedient involvement.

Miracle or Magic?

If I am being honest, most of the time I don't really want a miracle. I want magic.

Too often, we want an "abracadabra" God, but God wants an active and obedient follower. We want a disconnected God who waves a magic wand and fixes problems with no effort on our part. God, on the other hand, wants to be in relationship *with* people.

We want God to send money out of the sky rather than having to cut up credit cards and live on a budget. We want supernatural healing from physical ailments, but not at the cost of changing eating habits or following an exercise regimen. We want to be used mightily in life-changing ministry, but not if it involves engaging in the spiritual disciplines necessary to give God a platform from which He can work.

We disguise laziness as humility and determine that we are too ordinary to possibly make a difference. No person has anything extraordinary to offer God that would make Him step back in awe and declare, "Well, look! That one is completed!" Rather, God says, "I made you this way. I will use your obedience." Offer God your ordinary day so He can add the "extra" for His *extra*ordinary miracle.

Without God, you *cannot*. Without you, God *will* not.

Ask yourself what miracle you need, or what He wants to see accomplished in or through your life. Ask Him what He requires from you before He accomplishes the miracle. Your job is not to search for the miracle, but to seek Jesus. As you obediently follow Him, you will see His supernatural works surrounding you. They may not involve raising the dead, but these "little things"— like producing more wine for a wedding ceremony—are little miracles that carry enormous lessons.

Jesus Extends the Joy

Nearby stood six stone water jars, the kind used by the Jews for ceremonial washing, each holding from twenty to thirty gallons. Jesus said to the servants, "Fill the jars with water"; so they filled them to the brim. Then he told them, "Now draw some out and take it to the master of the banquet." They did so, and the master of the banquet tasted the water that had been turned into wine. He did not realize where it had come from, though the servants who had drawn the water knew. Then he called the bridegroom aside and said, "Everyone brings out the choice wine first and then the cheaper wine after the guests have had too much to drink; but you have saved the best till now." What Jesus did here in Cana of Galilee was the first

COLORS OF HOPE · 27

of the signs through which he revealed his glory; and his disciples believed in him. — **John 2:6–11 (NIV)**

Like those empty stone wine-jars, there are people and situations encircling you that have the potential to carry the miracle you need in your life. The servants at the wedding simply obeyed. The Scriptures say that "obedience is better than sacrifice (1 Samuel 15:22 NLT). The servants obeyed wholeheartedly, filling the jars "to the brim" (John 2:7 ESV). They were completely invested in following Him.

What if we also gave everything to Jesus? What if, when He gives us a direction, we give Him our unreserved best? What if we were to respond like these servants who thought their job was bussing tables at a wedding but were needed for something far greater—supporting roles in the best-selling book of all-time! (Not the one in your hands, mind you, but the Bible—though I can dream, right?) When we obey, we get a chance to be on the frontline of a miracle of God.

Notice that Jesus then gave them *His* best. He didn't make just any wine, but the *best* wine, and more than enough. Though this was near the end of the feast, Jesus made the party more enjoyable. And more importantly, by making the wine last longer, He prevented the family's name from being dishonored.

Jesus extends joy. Jesus saves the best for last. No matter where you are on your journey with Him, He has more for you. It is never too late for a miracle.

Chapter 1 Questions

Question: In what ways do you welcome Jesus in your life? What is one aspect of your life in which you could be more inviting to Jesus—and what will be your first step to grow in this area?

_____

_____

_____

_____

_____

_____

_____

_____

_____

_____

_____

_____

_____

_____

Question: In which areas of your life do you tend to try to keep to yourself or otherwise hold back from engaging with other people? What is one way in which you could engage more fully with others in your life—whether at home, at work, at school, or in your community?

_____

_____

_____

_____

_____

_____

_____

_____

_____

Question: What are some specific ways in which you can begin reaching out to others in love?

_____

_____

_____

_____

_____

_____

_____

_____

Action: Invite Jesus into your life! Then, step out in faith and engage with other people so you can show them God's love.

Chapter 1 Notes

COLORS OF HOPE · 31

CHAPTER TWO

Waiting on God's Way

The miracle at the wedding in Cana strengthened Jesus' disciples' faith, but also revealed His heart for people. Through an *ordinary* event, Jesus performed an *extraordinary* miracle: He turned water to wine, but more
importantly, preserved a family's honor.

This miracle was only the beginning of Jesus' supernatural work. His next miracle involved the healing of a
royal official's son. The man was not identified, but because of the way John referred to him, it is likely he was
a Jewish religious official—probably wealthy and with
some degree of authority among the people.

The man lived in Capernaum, where Jesus ministered
extensively, but at this point, Jesus was still in Cana. Capernaum was twenty-five miles of rough travel away.
The official's son was extremely ill, and the anxious father had likely exhausted all of the limited options that
his money and authority could provide.

As a father of four children, I understand this kind of
desperation. My twelve-year-old daughter and I were

recently having a discussion during our Bible reading, and she asked me a rather difficult question: "Dad, what really makes you afraid?"

I had not considered that question in some time, to be honest. We live a pretty safe life in a protected community, and my faith has come to a level where fear is not my greatest obstacle to life. (Krispy Kreme donuts are my greatest obstacle, but that's a whole nutha' story for a whole nutha' book.)

So, I sat there for a moment before the very first answer popped in my brain and out my mouth: "You or one of the other kids getting sick and dying," I said. Probably not the best thing to tell you daughter right before she goes to bed—now to dream horrible twelve-year-old type dreams about impending death. Dad of the year right here!

But it's true. If you are a parent, you know. There is not much worse that could happen to me than for something to happen to one of my kids.

If you have lost a child, you know what the royal official was feeling and experiencing. This man heard that Jesus was in tow, and he had heard just enough about Jesus that he ran to Him for help.

Miracles, Magic, and the Mundane

The man's son was close to death. When He learned that Jesus was in the area, Scripture says, "he went to Him and pleaded with Him to come down and heal his son" (John 4:47 HCSB).

When people need a miracle, they are willing to work. When they want magic, they are hoping for a show. This man was desperate and broken. This man's despair caused him to work—to travel to Jesus—because he needed a miracle.

Desperation often is the precursor to a miracle.

I find that often people run away from God in a crisis or try to fix things on their own. Sometimes they are ashamed because the crisis is a result of their own poor decisions. Ashamed, they try to hide from God and His people. However, this man was not ashamed. He went to *Jesus*—not as a last resort, but as the first support. He didn't hide from God, but ran to God.

The crowd probably knew who this official was. They were likely surprised this VIP would ask Jesus for anything, especially personal help. They were curious how Jesus would respond, and no doubt hoped for a little "abracadabra."

Jesus responded with a blunt but necessary statement:

Unless you people see signs and wonders, you will not believe. — **John 4:47–48 (HCSB)**

What Jesus was reminding us of, here, was that a faith built only on miracles will not withstand the mundane.

Sometimes you must walk through life doing the same things over and over again. You have to keep being faithful in what God has given you to do, and wait to see how He is going to use you. If your faith is built on miracles, you won't be able to weather the seasons of monotony.

You have to keep taking steps toward what author Eugene Peterson calls "a long obedience in the same direction," being faithful and obedient for the long haul in relationships and responsibilities.[4]

Jesus wants Christians to believe in Him whether they see a miracle or not. He told the crowd—and tells people today—"You say you believe in me and follow me, but really, you people just want to see another magic trick."

One of the things on which people come to me for advice, as a pastor, is knowing God's will. They want God to direct their steps regarding which school to attend, what job to pursue, which house to live in, or whom to marry. But what I have found to be true is that God's will isn't just about big decisions or major events. He prizes obedience in the mundane.

God made you unique from anyone else, and His will is that you would be the best you can be in day-to-day life—an excellent spouse, parent, employee, and follower of Christ. The mundane can also sometimes find us in a place of feeling stuck, unable to see movement, which brings on despair.

When It Really Matters

I am not sure that despair is a bad thing. Despair draws people to Jesus because they know they have no other options. In a world full of options, we need a little despair to remind us of the blank canvas of pain waiting to become a masterpiece in our lives.

This royal official sought out Jesus for a miracle. He pushed in and pleaded with Jesus: "Sir, come down before my boy dies!" (John 4:49 HCSB). This father didn't care what the crowd was there to see; he approached Jesus because he had nowhere else to go. He believed Jesus was who He said He was, and that He could help his son. His position and beliefs as a religious leader stood in sharp conflict with what he had heard about Jesus— but his son was dying and religion wasn't going to save his boy. He knew he needed something more.

One truth about pain is that faith becomes evident to a person when something that matters personally is threatened.

Religion can draw a person to church every Sunday, or at least make them a good "Chreaster" (that is, Christmas and Easter attender). But when a significant, emotional experience interrupts a person's life— resulting in a real, desperate need and real, debilitating pain—religion doesn't cut it. They need a real Savior!

Are you there now?

Come, Lord Jesus, before my marriage ends.

Come, Lord Jesus, before my health fails.

Come, Lord Jesus, before my dream dies.

Come, Lord Jesus, before this friendship withers.

Come, Lord Jesus, before my finances collapse.

You need a faith that is not built on a show, not built on magic, not even built on miracles, but is built on the person of Jesus!

God Has a Different Way

One would expect to read that Jesus responded by changing His plans and re-routing to Capernaum. However—unbelievably—Jesus told the man to return home, assuring him, "your son will live" (John 4:50a NIV).

What a tough answer to accept! Can you imagine this man's thoughts when Jesus said "no"? It had to feel like the bottom had truly dropped out of his hopes for his son's healing.

However, when Jesus says "no," it is because He has something better in mind. We pray for a certain job, a dramatic healing, or a financial turnaround. We invite Jesus into *our* plans and tell Him *how* we want Him to act. But God has a better way. And sometimes His way involves the answer "no." Perhaps the twenty-five-mile journey home was to help the official accept God's way over his way.

But I like consistency and fairness. So, when I read in Mark 5 that Jesus said "yes" to another man after saying "no" to the official, and that Jesus went with the second dad to heal his child, I feel for the first father. Why would Jesus go to one house and not the other?

Perhaps you wonder something similar:

Why do young couples find a marriage partner straight out of college, an answer to their prayer, but I am in my forties and still single?

Why do my friends seem to be getting every promotion like it's their destiny, yet I can't seem to catch a break?

One person's miracle does not have to look like everyone else's miracle. I guess in the end, it is critical to ask ourselves: What do we really want? Do we want magic, a miracle, or Jesus?

Did this man in John 4 want Jesus to go to Caperna-um? Or did he want his son healed? It's easy to become tangled in the "how" of the miracle and miss that God may have a different way for your life. He is not always going to do things the same way for you as He did for someone else because He is a relational God and He knows what *you* need.

Jesus knew that a twenty-five-mile journey home alone was what this official needed for his faith to be strengthened. The most important thing going on that day was not the child's healing, but the development of the official's soul and his heart. Sometimes one ordinary experience is preparation for what God has next. It's not about the miracle but about walking through the mundane.

I have always wanted a great marriage. My wife Connie and I have one, but it didn't evolve to this point in the precise way I thought it would. It came with endless learning, plenty of pain, and grace-filled miracles.

I always wanted to be a dad of a large family. We have three biological children, but we have been able to parent ten other children through foster care. We adopted our fourth child, and the future holds even more.

I wanted God to use me to plant a church. I thought the dream was dead but saw it revived in an unusual way. Then the dream died again. But the seed that had been planted twenty-four years earlier in my heart came to life, and now Freedom Church exists in a different way than I had ever dreamed.

You may have a vision for what you believe God is going to do in your life. Keep going on your "twenty-five-mile journey" back home. Remember what Jesus told you. Keep taking the next step forward. Keep obeying in the mundane. Don't grow weary, for God promises "at the proper time we will reap a harvest if we do not give up" (Galatians 6:9 NIV).

The Long Walk Home

Rather than questioning Jesus, the official began the journey home. Scripture says he "believed what Jesus said to him and departed" (John 4:50b HCSB). He didn't pitch a fit, rant and rave, give a list of demands, or use his position to try to force Jesus to Capernaum. His belief was not based on feeling, but on action. Every step home was another step of belief. Temporal faith depends on what God has recently done. Obedient, growing faith is what precedes a miracle.

It was a long trip back. Can you imagine the questions the likely swirled around in his mind? *Why did Jesus say no? Do I really trust Him and His plan, or am I just looking for what I can get out of this? Am I a man of faith who can courageously do whatever God puts before me?*

Before he arrived home, his slaves intercepted him with good news: his boy was alive! When the stunned father asked his servants when his son improved, their answer rattled all who were present:

> "Yesterday at seven in the morning the fever left him," they answered. The father realized this was the very hour at which Jesus had told him, "Your son will live."

Then he himself believed, along with his whole
household. — **John 4:52–53 (HCSB)**

The royal official had sought out Jesus. He took Jesus
at His word and put feet to his faith by heading home as
he was instructed. He believed in who Jesus was and received a wonderful miracle healing for his beloved as a
bonus to his own changed heart and transformed family.

Just like the official, God will always ask you to take
more steps than is comfortable—but He will also encourage you before you expect it.

The more often you obey Jesus, the stronger your
faith will grow and the easier it will be to trust Him in
the future. Remember the times Jesus has shown up in
your life—the blessings and favor He has already given
you. God's miracle for you today is also His encourage-
ment for you tomorrow.

But His miracle for you today is also your story for
others. The official's faith impacted his entire family,
and they too believed and followed Jesus. Your faith and
your miracle may be the miracle for someone else. Everything you go through is for a reason and will enable
you to be used by God as part of His grand plan to reach
a lost world.

Who do you know who is far from God but close to
you? What if God brought you to the place you are at
right now, so that you could be the miracle in their life?
Perhaps your journey of wrestling with doubt and learning to obey in the mundane was to bring them back to a
right relationship with God.

Though there may be pain in the process, rejoicing follows.

Chapter 2 Questions

Question: What are the "little," mundane aspects of your everyday life in which you think you generally do well in obeying God? In which of the mundane things could you improve in obedience—and what is your first step to growth in this area?

_____

_____

_____

_____

_____

_____

_____

_____

_____

_____

_____

_____

Question: What was a moment or incident in your past when you didn't understand what God was doing at first, but later came to appreciate His working in your life?

_____

_____

_____

_____

_____

_____

_____

_____

_____

Question: What is an example of working for a miracle instead of just wishing for one?

_____

_____

_____

_____

_____

_____

_____

_____

_____

Action: Obey God even in the mundane, everyday things—even when you don't understand His working in your life. Trust Him and be willing to labor for a miracle, instead of merely wishing for a quick fix.

Chapter 2 Notes

_____

_____

_____

_____

_____

_____

_____

_____

_____

_____

_____

_____

_____

_____

_____

_____

_____

_____

_____

_____

_____

_____

_____

_____

CHAPTER THREE

Picking Up Your Mat

Physical ailments can be debilitating, even if they are small. If you have ever broken your pinky toe, you know that injuring this ugly little body part can prevent a person from being able to walk!

Sometimes Jesus performed miracles that involved physical healing. But what He healed physically was a cover-up for something deeper. Jesus was continually looking to heal people spiritually. He was more interested in the colors of hope that would be left than the canvas of pain that He found.

John described one such miracle in compelling detail:

Afterward Jesus returned to Jerusalem for one of the Jewish holy days. Inside the city, near the Sheep Gate, was the pool of Bethesda, with five covered porches. Crowds of sick people—blind, lame, or paralyzed—lay on the porches. One of the men lying there had been sick for thirty-eight years." — **John 5:1–5 (NLT)**

Day after day, this paralyzed man came to the pool with the hope of being healed. He spread out his mat and crawled onto it the best he could in his condition. That was the space he lived in. It was the life he led, day after day, for thirty-eight years. This had been the story of this man's life for almost as long as I've been alive (as I write this chapter, I am forty-three years old).

The mat had become this man's life. The mat was all he knew. He couldn't walk away from it. He knew everything about the mat and how to survive on it. The mat came to symbolize the monotony and misery of his life—all there was and all there ever would be. He had accepted the mat.

It's one thing to be paralyzed physically, but sometimes we become paralyzed in other ways. We may be in a place of "I don't want to get up" or "I don't think I *can* get up." It's the familiar misery of what people do.

Perhaps you're paralyzed in your marriage. You're tired of trying and have settled into mat living, with no hope that it will ever improve. Maybe you are single for a season, but you've given up on finding a godly mate with whom you can share your life. Some are single for a reason and have taken on the mat of "divorce" or "adultery" as their identity. Some people are paralyzed with unforgiveness.

The mat feels safe to the— a place where they can't be hurt again. They are so busy crying out, "You have no idea how much they hurt me, Jesus," that they don't even realize they are stuck on a mat!

What is paralyzing you emotionally, spiritually, physically, or logistically? And how will you respond when Jesus comes along?

Jesus knew the paralytic had been ill for a long time. Seeing the man, Jesus asked, "Would you like to get well?'" (John 5:6 NLT). That's an important question. Do you really want to get well?

Sometimes people enjoy the mat. It becomes a security blanket that allows for selfishness and a righteous excuse. They don't really want to be healed. So Jesus asked this man if he was serious about being healed.

I think the word "well" was a loaded word for Jesus— it meant much more than simply being made "better." Jesus wasn't asking, "Do you want to walk," or even, "Do you want to be healed?"

He was asking the man if he wanted to be "whole," which is the meaning of the Greek work "well."[5] By asking if the man wanted to be well, then, Jesus was offering complete healing of the man's physical and spiritual being.

If the man had focused on his mat, he might have missed the miracle. And if you focus on the monotony and misery of life, you may miss a miracle, too.

God Sees You

When Jesus approached the pool of Bethesda, He did not see five porches full of people—He saw one person. Sometimes the greatest opportunity for a miracle begins with believing that Jesus sees you. He knows you. When you begin to comprehend His love for you, regardless of what your "mat" is, you are prepped for a miracle.

Perhaps you feel like no one sees you. You are surrounded by people, but you don't think anyone even cares. You feel alone and isolated in your pain.

But be encouraged! You are not alone. *God sees you, and is with you right now.* He sees you and knows you and understands you, even when no one else does.

There was a system at this pool of which everyone was aware. When the water began to bubble, those who could dip into the water could be healed. But this man did not have anyone to help him. Month after month, year after year, no one assisted him.

Sometimes the blessing is so close—like the Israelites wandering in the wilderness a few miles from the Promised Land—yet there is no apparent hope for arriving at the place of blessing.

Think about this: for thirty-eight years, this man was unable to convince anyone to help him. He had not one friend interested in seeing him healed. Was he an unkind, mean man? Did he have an entitlement attitude that turned people away? Had he completely given up on asking people for help and accepted his life for what it was?

Maybe the problem you are in is of your own making, at least partly, and Jesus wants to change *you* so *you* can change your problem. Regardless of how you arrived at your mat and what is keeping you there, Jesus sees you, and He is ready to work on your behalf.

How's That Working for You?

Though Jesus was ready to heal the paralytic, two words characterized the paralytic's attitude toward being healed: *I can't.*

When asked if he wanted to be made well, the man answered Jesus, "I can't, sir" (John 5:7 NLT). He proceeded to tell Jesus there was no one to put him into the pool when the water bubbled up—someone always stepped in ahead of him (John 5:7).

Have you ever said, "I can't"?

I can't get over this hurt.

I can't get past this paralysis.

I can't forgive my friend.

God, I know You want me to be walking in freedom and ministering to others, but I just can't.

What the paralyzed man was doing was not working. This man had seen miracles for other people time after time while he remained unchanged, yet he was still clinging to the same broken strategy.

Your financial "management" system which includes no budget, no giving, and no savings—how is that working for you?

The rut you are in with your wife, where you do not offer affection, do not help around the house, and do not spend time with her—how is that working for you?

Your walk with God that is void of passion, does not prioritize spending time with Him, and is not committed to a church family—how is that working for you?

Isn't it time to stop the insanity of doing the same thing expecting different results and instead try something different?

The Mat of Ministry

Jesus could see past this man's excuse, so He told him, "Stand up, pick up your mat, and walk!" (John 5:8 NLT). Scripture says the man was healed instantly: "He rolled up his sleeping mat and began walking!" (John 5:9).

He had never tried looking to God to heal him. Perhaps he could have been healed years before if he had been willing to trust God.

Jesus told the paralytic to pick up his mat. A person's natural inclination in this situation would be to leave the mat behind because it's no longer needed. I love what my friend Larry Bray says of the mat: "Jesus can transform a person's mat from a mat of misery and monotony to a mat of miracles—and the mat can then become their ministry!"

The burden of your past can be the blessing of someone else's future. The mat will become evidence of the work God has done in you, leading you to declare, "This is the situation God carried me through."

No longer a mat of shame, it will become a mat of strength. Somebody out there needs to see you carrying the mat—because the only way you can *carry* a mat is to have it in your hands, and the only way you can have it in your hands is to be up off the mat and *walking*! Somebody needs to know that you have been healed from an addiction so they will be encouraged to turn to Jesus to heal them of their addition. Somebody needs to see you free from bitterness so they can be healed from bitterness, too.

The mat will testify that Jesus has worked a miracle in your life.

There's also a camaraderie in the mat. C.S. Lewis said, "Friendship is born at the moment when one person says to another: 'What? You too? I thought I was the only one.'"[6] When people see you carrying your mat, they begin to identify with you. The end of your healing may be the beginning of someone else's miracle. Jesus said, "Get up!"

It's time to get up out of your loss.

It's time to get up out of your failure.

It's time to get up out of your monotony.

It's time to get up out of your fear.

It's time to get up and walk!

WORKBOOK

Chapter 3 Questions

Question: What's not working in your life right now, that you need to hand over to God?

_____

_____

_____

_____

_____

_____

_____

_____

_____

_____

Question: In your particular circumstance, what would it mean to leave this "mat" behind? What would it mean to pick up your mat and walk?

_____

_____

_____

_____

_____

_____

_____

_____

_____

_____

Question: What first steps will you take to pick up this "mat" in your life and move forward in faith?

_____

_____

_____

_____

_____

_____

_____

_____

_____

Action: Pick up your mat and walk! Don't stick to what's not working for you, and don't wallow in your past struggles. Instead, turn your mat of shame into a mat of strength that glorifies God! When you encounter difficulties in your daily life, great or small, trust that God sees you and is prepared to work on your behalf.

Chapter 3 Notes

CHAPTER FOUR

His Presence in the Storm

Perhaps you know from experience how quickly a storm can come up over a lake or river. One minute you are sailing under blue skies, and the next you are waiting out a squall that seems to have landed right on top of you.

And perhaps you have also experienced how quickly a storm can come up in life. One meeting with your boss. One phone call. One conversation with your spouse. One test result. Sometimes just one word, and everything changes.

This is what happened to Jesus' disciples. They had spent the day ministering with Him and were exhausted. They had watched him miraculously multiply some loaves of bread and a few fish into enough food to feed five thousand. The Bible says they next climbed aboard a boat and set sail on the Sea of Galilee:

> When evening came, his disciples went down to the lake, where they got into a boat and set off across the lake for Capernaum. By now it was dark, and Jesus

had not yet joined them. A strong wind was blowing and the waters grew rough. When they had rowed about three or four miles, they saw Jesus approaching the boat, walking on the water; and they were frightened." — **John 6:16–19 (NIV)**

John said that "they saw Jesus" (John 6:19) but Matthew and Mark's accounts reveal the disciples believed they had seen a ghost—which alarmed them (Matthew 14:26, Mark 6:49). Other translations say they were "terrified."

And honestly, would you not had been terrified, too? Let's cut these guys a little slack. I think if someone walked past me on the water, I might blurt out a choice phrase or two, at least in my head.

Seeing a miracle like walking on water opens a slew of deep issues that human minds have a hard time processing. Sometimes the supernatural is frightening because people think supernatural activity can only be done by something that should be feared. The disciples were witnessing a supernatural move of God, but they thought it was a spook from the enemy—and were fearful.

Often God begins to answer prayers in supernatural ways, but instead of rejoicing, fear of what the answer may mean or the power that has made it happen takes over.

This is what happened to the disciples as they were tossed back and forth on the sea—instead of trusting God, they feared the power of the storm. However, Jesus was not unaware, and He spoke comfort to His terrified friends:

But he said to them, "It is I; don't be afraid." Then they
were willing to take him into the boat, and immediately
the boat reached the shore where they were heading.
— **John 6:20–21 (NIV)**

At first glance, it may appear the problem was
solved—the boat reached the shore and the disciples
were safe. However, Jesus had a deeper purpose for everything that He had just done, including the miracle of
walking on water. These miracles were called signs, because they pointed to the truth. Jesus had two purposes
for walking on the water: to show His power and to reveal His presence.

His Power: He Is God

Jesus' divinity was a truth the disciples still didn't
understand, even after Jesus had just fed five thousand
people. The disciples were out in the middle of an eight-
mile-wide lake. On a normal day, it would take four
hours to row across it. It was the fourth watch of the
night, which was between 3 a.m. and 6 a.m.[7] According
to my calculations (and I admit that I have never been
strong at math), if the disciples had set out right after
dinner, they had most likely been rowing for nearly eight
hours, twice as long as it should have taken—and they
were still in the middle of the lake!

Jesus did not come to their rescue right away, though
He could have. The disciples rowed against the waves
for many hours before Scripture says He "meant to pass
by them" (Mark 6:48 ESV). Jesus' timing was intentional. Jesus always shows up at just the right time.

This storm was really a picture of the storm going on in their hearts and minds. The questions with which the disciples were likely struggling are the same questions many struggle with today: Where are You, Jesus? Do You see we are stuck, unable to row through this storm? Who are You, Jesus, and why haven't You come to our rescue?

The Gospel of Mark revealed additional insight into this miracle. John said Jesus was not with them, but Mark included the reason why: "Immediately Jesus made his disciples get into the boat and go on ahead of him to Bethsaida, while he dismissed the crowd. After leaving them, he went up on a mountainside to pray" (Mark 6:45–46 NIV).

It was a set up. Jesus pushed the disciples ahead and went to seek after God alone, knowing full well that there would be a storm. One translation refers to this time as "meanwhile." You know what "meanwhile" means. It's the time when you are obeying God (the disciples were doing exactly what Jesus had told them) and you are on your way to somewhere (they knew their destination) and yet the storm still comes.

"Meanwhile" is the time of waiting. Waiting to hear from God. Waiting to learn the lesson. Meanwhile stinks. But in this passage, we see that Jesus had something for the disciples to learn in the meanwhile.

Sometimes in this period of time known as "meanwhile," God will lead you into a period of loneliness or struggle to refocus on Him—just as He allowed the disciples to labor for some time before He appeared on the water:

Later that night, the boat was in the middle of the lake, and he was alone on land. He saw the disciples straining at the oars, because the wind was against them. — **Mark 6:47–48a (NIV)**

The disciples were physically and spiritually worn out but Mark wrote "He saw." Jesus was watching.

This is such a great statement of hope! Jesus sees His people's struggles. He cares about their struggles.

At just the right time, the specific and intentional time of Jesus, He made His presence known to the disciples. Mark 6:48b says, "Shortly before dawn he went out to them, walking on the lake. He was about to pass by them" (NIV).

Did you notice the gap? "Later that night" Jesus saw them from the land, but it was "shortly before dawn" that Jesus went out to them. If I were John, Mark, or Matthew (who each documented this account), I would have asked Jesus, "Wait, what? Jesus, You saw us struggle and You stayed on dry land—*for a few more hours*?"

Yes. He allowed them to struggle while He watched. God sees you struggling, too. He sees you wrestling with that same sin kicking your tail, stuck in those old habits. God sees your marriage unraveling as you cry out to Him. God sees as you make no progress in your fight against addiction. God sees you desperately trying to make ends meet. God sees you in the storm, but He is not nearly as concerned with your comfort as He is with your character.

The storm going on inside Jesus' disciples was far more important than the storm on the lake. But Jesus used the external storm as a tool to help settle the storm inside. It was a momentary setback to enable a much bigger work He wanted to do.

When in the gap between "later that night" and "shortly before dawn," it's easy to say, "I'm waiting on God." But how often is *He* waiting on *you*? Notice that Mark's account says, "He was about to pass by them" (Mark 6:48 NIV). Jesus was not walking on water to go rescue them, but because He needed to be at the other side for the next part of His ministry!

How many times has God passed you by, not because He did not have a miracle ready for you, but because *you* were not ready for the miracle? If you are fighting against God's plan for developing your character, you may miss His presence.

His Presence

When the disciples set out in the boat that evening, they thought they were big and powerful. They weren't concerned with the fact that Jesus was not with them. They didn't say, "We can't do this without You," or "We want to stay and pray with You." They were heady from the miracle of the multiplication of the loaves and fishes they had participated in and the resulting crowd's enthusiasm. They were perfectly willing to go on without the presence of God. They were so puffed up on themselves and their success in ministry that He allowed them to grow hungry again. The presence of God is better than any strategy or any success.

When the storm came, the disciples were terrified. Sometimes it takes being terrified without Jesus to begin to realize a need for Him. Desperation is good, but hunger must be filled the right way.

For example, to satisfy his ravenous hunger, Esau traded his identity and future for a cup of soup (Genesis 25:33–34). People often try to stop their gnawing need with momentary pleasure instead of seeking God's presence. A little more money. A little sexual escapade. A momentary fix on the computer. "Fill me up, because I'm hungry!" people cry with Esau.

But God says, "Wait! I'm making you into something." Be so ravenous for *His presence* that you are terrified to move without it.

The disciples had arrived at the place God wanted them to be—desperately dependent on Him. Jesus was on the way to the other side of the lake. He was walking on water, not to do a miracle, but because that is what God does. The real miracle was what happened in the disciples' lives. Jesus was demonstrating His power and His divinity. He is always God and is always in control over the water and any storm. But His power only becomes a miracle at the point of need—when one of His children realizes they need Him.

The disciples were at that point. Notice how Jesus responds:

Immediately he spoke to them and said, "Take courage! It is I. Don't be afraid." Then he climbed into the boat with them, and the wind died down. They were completely amazed, for they had not understood about the loaves; their hearts were hardened.
— **Mark 6:50–52 (NIV)**

Isn't it amazing how shocked people are upon realizing God continues to be God? The disciples should have been praying, "God, do it again!" after witnessing such a great miracle just hours before. Perhaps human forgetfulness is why God calls people to "remember" so many times throughout the pages of the Bible. Consider what God did when He took you through a previous storm. Remember, and be encouraged.

There is a great old Puritan saying: "The same sun which melts the wax, hardens the clay."[8] Jesus, who performs miracles, also allows for struggle. The disciples saw Jesus miraculously break the loaves so hungry people would be filled. They didn't understand that Jesus Himself was the bread of life, and He Himself had to be broken so hungry souls would be satisfied. Move beyond seeking the *power* of Jesus to hungering for the *presence* of Jesus.

Understanding the "why" instead of just the "what" is the first step to experiencing Jesus. The disciples understood Jesus had power, but didn't understand He *was* power. They understood Jesus was from God, but didn't understand Jesus Himself *was* God. The sign is only there to point to the destination. Don't miss Jesus by chasing after the miracle.

Are you struggling against the wind in your life? Perhaps you are trying to move forward but are disobeying God's instruction. Perhaps you are rowing without reaching a destination, like the disciples—frustrated in your marriage or with parenting, in your finances or vocation—and looking for the miracle.

The disciples walked with Jesus for three years, constantly hearing His teaching and observing His kingdom work. However, they still missed who He was. It is possible to be around Jesus continually without ever really knowing Him.

So often in life's storms, while we're wondering why something is happening and agonizing over what to do, God is teaching us something much bigger—to rest in who He is and leave the unsearchable to Him. To *know* Him.

In the midst of the disciples' lack of understanding and hard hearts, Jesus walked on water. He defied the laws of the universe that He created, wordlessly telling them, "I am God." Stop looking for God to walk on water, but instead, look for *Him*.

Long for His presence more than any protection or provision and you will make it through even the toughest storm.

Chapter 4 Questions

Question: What worries are distracting you from God?

_____

_____

_____

_____

_____

_____

_____

_____

_____

_____

_____

Question: How, specifically, can you refocus on God instead of on these worries?

_____

_____

_____

_____

_____

_____

_____

_____

_____

_____

_____

_____

_____

Question: What does it mean, specifically, to desire God's presence in your life? How can you express your desire for His presence and your trust in His providence?

_____

_____

_____

_____

_____

_____

_____

_____

_____

_____

_____

_____

Action: Instead of focusing on life's storms and worrying about what to do, focus on God. Desire and expect His presence, and trust that His protection and providence will follow.

Chapter 4 Notes

CHAPTER FIVE

Miracle in the Mess

The next miracle of Jesus occurs in John 9 and involves a man who had been blind from birth. This man had never *not* been blind. He had never seen the faces of those he loved and who loved him. He had never seen the sun setting over Jerusalem, the flowers on the Judean countryside, or the mountain landscape.

In Mark 10, Jesus healed a different blind man named Bartimaeus. Scripture says he "regained" his sight, which means he received it back. He knew what he was missing—he knew as he cried out "Have mercy on me!" (Mark 10:48 ESV) that he needed healing, and he knew how great this miracle would be.

But the man in John's account only knew what he knew—total blindness. He had never been able to see. His canvas of pain was blank, but he had no idea of what vibrant colors could look like.

Like this man, you only know what you know. Perhaps you've never seen a good marriage. Never had an example of good parenting. Never had any self-worth confirmed in your heart or anticipation for your future built into your soul.

When Jesus shows up, He shines a light on the darkest places of your life—places where you are blind to what you are missing. With His light, there is hope and a future and a difference.

Who's to Blame?

It's in our nature to blame others. If you have children or have ever been around a child (or still act like a child yourself) you know this is true. It's often a defense mechanism to protect oneself—but in truth it's an avoidance of one's own fault or sin. People excuse themselves for the same negative behavior for which they blame others.[9]

One day as the disciples walked with Jesus, this issue of blame bubbled to the surface:

> As Jesus was walking along, he saw a man who had been blind from birth. "Rabbi," his disciples asked him, "why was this man born blind? Was it because of his own sins or his parents' sins?" — **John 9:1–2 (NLT)**

It does not take a rocket scientist to know if the man was born blind, he did not commit punishable sin in the womb. So then, was this a punishment for his parents? Like many people, the disciples were looking for someone to blame. When folks come into counseling with me, one of the first questions I ask is, "Why are we here?" It's interesting to hear the responses, from those who always blame themselves for everything that has gone wrong in their lives, to couples in troubled marriages who look at each other and point like two toddlers— "They did it!"

But Jesus replied "no" to all their assumptions. He said, "It was not because of his sins or his parents' sins … This happened so the power of God could be seen in him" (John 9:3 NLT).

The reason this man was born blind was so He could heal him, Jesus declared. In essence, He said, "The reason he has gone through this life never having seen, the reason someone has to lead him to this place every morning, and the reason he's never been employed and must beg to survive, is so I could heal him. The reason he is distant from people, unable to enjoy relationships and partake in life the way they can, and the reason he's had this constant struggle and burden every single day of his entire life, is so that I could come today and restore his sight. It's all so God could be glorified."

That about was as awesome for the blind man who lived two thousand years ago as it would be for someone in my church—not very awesome at all. When a struggle comes into *my* life, I don't immediately see the potential beauty of what God might be doing.

Instead, I typically cry, "God, what did I do? Why, God, are You punishing me after how I've been walking with You?"

Suddenly, doubts surface about God's character, or even His existence. I find myself wrestling with this a little—or a lot.

Ultimately, we must face this difficult truth: sometimes we must go through tough circumstances so God can display His glory in our lives. The good news is that God's glory works to our own benefit as well.

God's Glory Displayed

What does it mean for God to display His glory? God's glory is the beauty that emanates from His nature—all of His attributes manifested together.[10] God revealed what these attributes are when He revealed His name to Moses. God proclaimed His character is "merciful and gracious, slow to anger, and abounding in steadfast love and faithfulness, keeping steadfast love for thousands, forgiving iniquity and transgression and sin, but who will by no means clear the guilty, visiting the iniquity of the fathers on the children and the children's children, to the third and the fourth generation" (Exodus 34:6–7 ESV).

God's glory—His nature—can be seen within believers, but it does not originate from them. It is of God.[11] This means your life is intended to be a mirror to a lost world, reflecting the image of who God really is.

There are two extreme theological arguments about the question of God's identity that cloud the issue. One theory translates God's all-powerful nature into the assertion that all evil is operating under God's control and approval. The problem with this claim is that it falsely credits God with responsibility for many terrible circumstances and events.

By contrast, the second argument suggests that evil is a result of God choosing to be disconnected from the world He created. However, this claim inaccurately presents evil as being outside of God's control, implying that God is not, in fact, all-powerful.

Both arguments protect people from actually dealing with the *real* question. The contrast is between theory and practical reality. It's easy when the question "Who is God?" remains someone else's opinion. It is much harder work to process the question when it becomes personal.

The truth is that comfort is not the most important thing to God—He is most concerned with character. Often a believer's calling comes out of personal suffering. God's work does not revolve around His people's pleasure. It is super-easy for me to write that, but just like you, I have an issue *accepting* it in times of not-so-theoretical pain.

Can you accept that the world revolves around God and not you? Can you embrace your suffering, your loss, or your burden as an opportunity to reflect the image of God to others?

There is a twelve-year-old boy in my church, named Riley, who has nephrotic syndrome, a severe kidney disorder. For most of his life, he's had to be on multiple strong medications. The steroids that help his body combat the effects of this disease also cause him to gain weight. He's been picked on and misunderstood by other kids his age.

Throughout his life, Riley has been in and out of the hospital, never knowing when his life will be interrupted again with another hospital stay. There's been physical pain as well as the emotional pain of knowing he does not have the freedom to go and do all the things that a healthy young man can do.

But I heard Riley say something one time that startled me and changed me: "God allowed me to have this disease so that I could reach out to the mission field of the others who have it." He is twelve. He is sick. He is strong. He understands God. And he is doing just that. He's a rock star to others with the disease and to the medical community that helps care for him.

At a young age, Riley has embraced his situation and uses the opportunity to reflect the image of God to others.

He offers a message of hope, despite his pain and hurt. The question is, do we?

When All Right Isn't All Right

When John the Baptist was captive in Herod's prison, about to be beheaded for obeying God's call on his life, he sent word to Jesus: "Are you the one who is to come, or shall we look for another?" (Matthew 11:3 ESV).

In modern language, John was saying, "Hey, this is not what I was expecting. Just wanted to check in. Call me when you get a chance. Maybe a text message, snapchat ... something." The other disciples were taking part in miracles and preaching the gospel while John was in chains. His ministry was over, and all earthly prospects were growing dimmer by the day.

Jesus' answer had to be a hard one to hear: "Tell John what you hear and see: the blind receive their sight and the lame walk, lepers are cleansed and the deaf hear, and the dead are raised up, and the poor have good news preached to them" (Matthew 11:4–5 ESV).

John would have immediately recognized Isaiah's prophecy about the Messiah in those words. He also would have understood that, out of love for his friend, Jesus didn't include Isaiah's phrase "proclaim liberty to the captives" (Isaiah 61:1 ESV). Jesus' promise for John, while not one of deliverance, would bring the peace John needed to sustain him for his difficult few days that remained.

Some things happen so that the glory of God can be revealed. Jesus was saying to John, "I *am* the Messiah. My glory is going to shine through this situation, but you are going to die."

Real talk? That doesn't jive with American Christianity, in which Christians so often believe if they follow Jesus, their life will be easy.

Real-er talk? I look to blame God when things don't work out the way I want. I often am guilty of thinking of Him as my spiritual butler. But the Bible teaches that what I want may look different from what God wants.

It doesn't matter what someone is born with; it matters that they can be born again. It doesn't matter what a person is going through; it matters what Jesus has already been through. It doesn't matter what the present holds, because all that matters is the future God has in store for those who believe.

God allows certain things to happen so that He can set a person right, whether miraculously right, as with this man born blind, or ultimately right, as with John the

Baptist. Whatever you are going through, God has a purpose and a plan!

Your Miracle May Look Like a Mess

Sometimes the manner in which Jesus sets a person right makes absolutely no sense to the logical mind. Jesus was about to restore the blind man's sight, but how He did it baffled those who were watching. Scripture says, "Then he [Jesus] spit on the ground, made mud with the saliva, and spread the mud over the blind man's eyes" (John 9:6 NLT).

This is probably not the way anyone would choose to see a miracle. When I think of Jesus hacking a throat pony and then mixing it up into a paste, I envision a mess. Sometimes your miracle may look chaotic, or not the way you envision it should be. This blind man was likely not hoping someone would smear spit on his eyes. But let's be honest: if you had been living your whole life in darkness, a little mess would be the least of your worries.

Sometimes you will have to work through a mess to arrive at a place of wholeness and healing. For example, almost all Christian parents would agree they want kids who are emotionally and spiritually healthier than they are—kids who are confident in who they are in Christ and ready to serve Him with their lives.

But parenting is messy. Your seven-year-old needs you to *teach* him character. Your little girl needs you to *show* her modesty. It's a lot easier to turn on another movie or hand them the iPad and not have to parent quite so much.

My wife and I have been blessed to be foster parents. We have the privilege of a moment in time in which we can give these precious children a glimpse of something they've never experienced. But it's a privilege that can be very messy, as we are two broken people taking part in a broken system and helping other very broken (little) people.

Here is a Facebook post that I wrote in June of 2015 that recounts this messiness:

I don't know if it's possible to feel stares. But if it is, I did on Sunday.

"The B Man," our most recent foster placement of just twelve days, was laying on the floor in Arby's— screaming. Loud.

I am not completely sure what made him feel unsafe and honestly in that moment it did not matter. Something did and he was now scared, or mad, or both.

So, I found myself lying on the floor at Arby's.

Fast food restaurant floors are gross by the way. That is just an aside.

"B," I say. "You are safe. Daddy is right here." (Yes, twelve days in and he calls me Daddy and since he has never called anyone else that to my knowledge we are going with it). I will stay here with you for a minute, but I am going to pick you up in just a moment if that's okay."

More screams. More really loud screams.

This is when I felt the heaviness of people's stares.

Stares that I have probably given before ... stares that bellow, "You just need to pick that child up and tell him this is not acceptable," or, "What kind of parent are you? You must be a permissive parent." Stares that communicate, "That kid gets away with anything."

I gently picked "B" up and he buried his head into my shoulder.

I walked slowly out of the restaurant into the heat outside.

He looked up at me and said, "Daddy, you mad at me?"

"No Buddy, I am not mad at all. I am protecting you. You are safe."

Smiles replaced screams.

God reminded me through this incident. Everyone has a story and we never know when someone's story is quite unexplainable. Like a child who has only been in a family for twelve days and just needs a little grace.

Rather than staring I think I will just help the next time I see a parent struggling. Even if that help is just to not stare.

Yet God's messy is better than my mundane any day. Too often, we try to limit God and how He might do what He is going to do. Subconsciously, we think we know best and have better ideas. There are times when we might think, "If God would just listen," rather than affirm, "I am listening, God."

Don't limit God. Let him be limitless.

Jesus continued His instruction to the blind man: "'Go wash yourself in the pool of Siloam' (Siloam means 'sent'). So, the man went and washed and came back seeing!" (John 9:7 NLT).

COLORS OF HOPE · 77

It is a sad reality that I should need to write any more about this story! There was a man who was born blind, but now could see. If you encountered that today, or if the next time you went to church someone who had been born blind suddenly gained their sight, you wouldn't sit back and cerebrally ask if he could teach you some lessons—maybe three things that start with the same letter so it's easy to remember—about healing. No, you and everyone around you would be ecstatic. You would worship and clap and praise and celebrate!

Here is the truth: miracles just as amazing as the blind man's sight happen all the time. But they are often missed.

Two people whose marriage was falling apart—a relationship that was nothing but a canvas of pain—may now be growing in true love for one another, filled with colors of hope.

Parents who did not know what to do with their children might now be seeing Jesus shining His light into their kids, who are growing and maturing spiritually.

Friendships that were absolutely crushed might be in the process of being restored. Souls that were strangled by addiction may now be walking in freedom. People who didn't know Jesus or walk intimately with Him are being baptized into a new life.

But people miss the miracle in the mess.

Whatever Jesus sees fit to happen is not just okay, it's best. With the best comes the blessing, and if you receive the blessing, you can deal with the burden.

Whatever you are going through, God's glory is bigger! If you don't let Jesus take you through the mess—if you wipe off your eyes and question God: "Who spit on me? What's going on?"—you may never see the bigger picture of God's glory.

WORKBOOK

Chapter 5 Questions

Question: When in your past has a messy situation turned out for the best?

_____

_____

_____

_____

_____

_____

_____

_____

_____

_____

_____

Question: What seems like a mess in your life right now?

_____

_____

_____

_____

_____

_____

_____

_____

_____

_____

_____

Question: How, specifically, can you let go of your worries about your own shortcomings so God can display His glory in your situation?

_____

_____

_____

_____

_____

_____

_____

_____

_____

_____

Action: Remember that miracles can be messy. Don't miss His miracles in the mess! During difficult or chaotic moments, remind yourself that He is less concerned with your comfort than with your well-being. Rejoice when His glory shines through your mess!

Chapter 5 Notes

_____

_____

_____

_____

_____

_____

_____

_____

_____

_____

_____

_____

_____

_____

_____

_____

_____

_____

_____

_____

_____

_____

_____

_____

_____

_____

_____

_____

CHAPTER SIX

Purpose in Pain

Pain is often the best professor. So often, people wish pain away, or feel it is pointless. Yet like an artist's blank canvas, pain is needed to allow color—the colors of hope—the space to form beautiful art. Pain is the starting point of our transformation. It reveals what each of us needs to become.

In short, pain is a fountain of discovery. It leads to understanding one's greater purpose and prepares a person to fulfill that purpose. Pain creates borders and edges in life and points to the good God is doing.

Don't despise a season of pain. Many times, it is both the indicator and the preparation for the next season's promise. Pain is the canvas on which God can paint with colors of hope.

The disciples were in a season of learning what it means to rest in Jesus, and the next step of their journey involved a interaction with a demon-possessed man. This man's life was turned upside down because of Jesus. His was a life filled with pain—and an unusual amount of trust.

Look to the One in Charge

This next miracle comes from Mark 5. But to set the scene, it's important to go back to the end of Mark 4, just before the disciples hopped into the boat to sail across the Sea of Galilee:

> As evening came, Jesus said to his disciples, "Let's cross to the other side of the lake." So they took Jesus in the boat and started out, leaving the crowds behind (although other boats followed). But soon a fierce storm came up. High waves were breaking into the boat, and it began to fill with water. Jesus was sleeping at the back of the boat with his head on a cushion. The disciples woke him up, shouting, "Teacher, don't you care that we're going to drown?"
> **— Mark 4:35–38 (NLT)**

As we saw in an earlier chapter, sometimes Christians must be willing to obey what they don't understand to receive what they can't comprehend. For the disciples, the idea of clamoring aboard a boat and heading into a storm after dark probably didn't make sense. As soon as believers make up their mind to follow Jesus, a storm always seems to pop up—and one of their first questions is often, "Where is God in this?"

The best thing you can do in a storm is look at the one in charge. This is my philosophy during turbulence on a plane: Look at the flight attendant!

One time I was on a propeller plane from South Bend, Indiana, to Chicago during a tornado outbreak. As the passengers were rushed onto the plane, we heard the words, "We've got to hurry or they aren't going to let us fly." I thought maybe we should listen to "them."

But the plane took off and almost immediately began bumping around in the air. Passengers were screaming. The co-pilot's voice came through the mic and suggested we pray. I am all about prayer, mind you, but that was one prayer request I would prefer not to have heard!

So I employed my philosophy and I looked at the flight attendant to gauge the seriousness of the situation. He was sitting, seatbelt on, head between his legs, sobbing like a little girl at a One Direction concert. (Substitute in "Michael Jackson concert" if you're in your fifties, or "Justin Bieber concert" if you're in in your thirties. I just want to be a relevant author who makes my illustrations stick. I also want to be an author who included Harry Styles, Michael Jackson, and Justin Bieber in my book.)

But back to the attendant—clearly, if ever there was a time to worry, this was it!

The disciples did right to take their fears to Jesus, but if they had really been taking their cues from the One in charge, they would have seen there was no reason to be afraid. Jesus was sleeping, not panicking.

When He woke up, the Bible says "He rebuked the wind and said to the waves, 'Silence! Be still!'" (Mark 4:39a NLT). Notice what happened next:

> Suddenly the wind stopped, and there was a great calm. Then he asked them, "Why are you afraid? Do you still have no faith?"

The disciples were absolutely terrified. "Who is this man?" they asked each other. "Even the wind and waves obey him!" — **Mark 4:39b–41 (NLT)**

So here is the question I have: What in the world did Jesus want the disciples to do? Were they to do nothing and wait for the storm to pass? Perhaps the storm was not that bad and they were overreacting.

Maybe, but I don't think so. No, I think Jesus was modeling for them what He wanted them to do—*rest*. Be at peace. Trust Him.

The disciples were so afraid, they forgot Jesus was with them. What Jesus expected them to do was to ask Him to take care of them—and even better, to *trust* Him to take care of them. Instead they doubted, likely playing out the worst-case scenario in their minds. They were convinced they were all going to die before they had even woken Jesus up!

How often do followers of Jesus do the same? The presence of Jesus dwells within everyone who believes. Yet when difficult times come, all too often we forget Jesus and give in to their fear. Fear can prevent people from seeing God and His good purposes.

Jesus had new opportunities for the disciples. They were about to witness a formidable and public miracle. But their fear shackled their future.

Fear can keep us from having the kind of faith that ushers in miracles.

Are you trusting Jesus in your pain, and trusting Him when His plan is different from yours? Sometimes Jesus will allow you to go through a storm because He has a divine appointment waiting that will unleash God's destiny for your life. Press through the fear, and focus on Jesus. Your faith just might usher in a miracle.

Living in a Dead Place

The disciples survived the storm—surely something awesome awaited them on the other side, right? Unfortunately, what is waiting on the other side of the storm isn't always easy:

> So they arrived at the other side of the lake, in the region of the Gerasenes. When Jesus climbed out of the boat, a man possessed by an evil spirit came out from the tombs to meet him. — **Mark 5:1–2 (NLT)**

The disciples climbed out of the boat and found themselves in a graveyard, where they were greeted by a naked zombie—or, at least, a man who might have looked and acted like one.

There is a crucial lesson to learn from this demon-possessed man's story. Just because someone is in a dead place does not mean they themselves are dead. You may be in a marriage, a church, or a vocational situation where you see no signs of life, no movement, or no light at the end of the tunnel. Perhaps you have been hanging out in the dead place so long you sometimes think you are dead yourself. You think you belong there.

However, for followers of Jesus, this is the farthest thing from the truth. Paul said in his letter to the Ephesians that before faith in Christ, "you were dead because of your disobedience and your many sins" (Ephesians 2:1 NLT). Yet this is not where Christians are now.

Paul continued and said that Jesus "raised us from the dead along with Christ and seated us with him in the heavenly realms because we are united with Christ Jesus" (Ephesians 2:6 NLT). Christ-followers have been made alive with Christ.

Those who have not yet believed in Jesus are in a much different place:

> This man lived in the burial caves and could no longer be restrained, even with a chain. Whenever he was put into chains and shackles—as he often was—he snapped the chains from his wrists and smashed the shackles. No one was strong enough to subdue him. Day and night he wandered among the burial caves and in the hills, howling and cutting himself with sharp stones. — **Mark 5:3–5 (NLT)**

The possessed man was in pain. He was lonely. He was harming himself. By cutting himself, he could *feel* something. As Nine-Inch-Nails so aptly wrote, "I hurt myself today, to see if I still feel."[12] I know that many of you have been there, believing that pain is acceptable if it reminds you of what it is like to feel again.

The possessed man was trying to control the uncontrollable, to gain a temporary freedom.

The interesting thing about this man is that he was in a constant pursuit of freedom—breaking away from the chains that held him, at times literally. He knew his destiny was to have the chains broken, but did not know who could bring him that freedom. He needed Jesus.

Jesus came to free people from sin—from things like addiction or illness, bitterness or anger. But sometimes a person will remain in pain because they are struggling.

They are fighting to find the freedom they know should be theirs. People cut themselves down emotionally, searching for an elusive freedom that only Jesus can provide.

Somehow the possessed man knew to seek out Jesus. In a lucid moment, when he saw Jesus from a distance, Scripture says he "ran to meet him, and bowed low before him" (Mark 5:6 NLT). Jesus was the first person to see *him* and not his demons, his condition, or his circumstances. Jesus was the first person to seek him out rather than avoiding him. This man's posture changed. He ran to meet Jesus, recognizing who He was and believing Jesus had all he needed.

This demon-possessed man's response was how Jesus wanted His disciples to react on the boat—not with panic, but with a posture that trusted Him to be Lord over their storm. The disciples could learn from this afflicted man. Those who have been prisoners know what freedom really is. Everyone needs the Savior, but some are more aware of their need than others.

Know Thine Enemy

The situation quickly took a darker turn when one of the spirits that possessed the man cried out:

> With a shriek, he screamed, "Why are you interfering with me, Jesus, Son of the Most High God? In the name of God, I beg you, don't torture me!" For Jesus had already said to the spirit, "Come out of the man, you evil spirit." Then Jesus demanded, "What is your name?" — **Mark 5:7–9a (NLT)**

Take a moment to name your enemies. When you consciously name them, you're unlikely to call a friend a foe by accident. And sometimes, we tend to lose perspective and get confused. We think our enemy is a political leader or party, a struggling friend, a boss, or a coworker. We may even consider their spouse, parents, or their kids to be enemies.

None of these are big enough to be the real enemy, however. Jesus didn't see this man as the enemy.

Sometimes Christ-followers begin to follow God in obedience until trouble comes into their lives and they wonder why the enemy is suddenly upon them. I can tell you why! We weren't a threat to Satan before—we were on his team. If Satan is not pushing against you, maybe it's because you are moving in the same direction.

Understand that there is an enemy after your soul. Peter wrote, "Stay alert! Watch out for your great enemy, the devil. He prowls around like a roaring lion, looking for someone to devour" (1 Peter 5:8 NLT). The enemy of your soul does not want your marriage, your friendships, your family, or your job to thrive. He is looking to devour *you*.

The enemy wanted to devour the man possessed by the evil spirits in Mark 5, too. However, Scripture reveals that the spirits possessing him were afraid of Jesus' power:

And he replied, "My name is Legion, because there are many of us inside this man." Then the evil spirits begged him again and again not to send them to some distant place. — **Mark 5:9b–10 (NLT)**

There is a spiritual battle inside of every person who follows Jesus, including you. It's a battle for your body and the physical actions you take. It's a battle for your soul—your emotions and thoughts. What will you think? What will you think on? What will you believe? What will you put in your body? What pleasures will you seek after?

And it's ultimately a battle for your spirit—for your connection with God. Your body, soul, and spirit work together. They are intertwined. And the spirit you feed the most will win.

If you give attention to your fears or your doubts, for example, they will take over. Starve your body from emotions that are not from God and let them know they are not in charge.

The spirits that possessed the man were not in charge of him. Jesus made this clear in an odd display that followed:

There happened to be a large herd of pigs feeding on the hillside nearby. "Send us into those pigs," the spirits begged. "Let us enter them." So Jesus gave them permission. The evil spirits came out of the man and entered the pigs, and the entire herd of about 2,000 pigs plunged down the steep hillside into the lake and drowned in the water. The herdsmen fled to the nearby town and the surrounding countryside, spreading the news as they ran. People rushed out to see what had happened. A crowd soon gathered around Jesus, and they saw the man who had been possessed by the legion of demons. He was sitting there fully clothed and perfectly sane, and they were all afraid.
— **Mark 5:11–15 (NLT)**

What is going on here?

I have no idea.

Even scholars who have examined this passage extensively can only guess. But here is the big-picture takeaway: Jesus had the power and right to do what He pleased. In this situation, He displaced those evil spirits from the man into a herd of pigs.

Whatever the enemy, whatever the battle, know this: Jesus has power over *whatever*. Whatever you face. Whatever you have done. Whatever your past has left in your wake. *Whatever*.

Why did Jesus use pigs? Perhaps it was to show that He is Lord over everything, even over one's possessions. This was the herdsmen's business and livelihood. When the pigs dropped of the ledge into the water, the herdsmen lost their business—*but a man was healed.*

When God starts to paint with colors of hope on your canvas of pain, other people will notice. It will draw a crowd. Perhaps Jesus put the demons in the pigs to gather the crowd to witness the restoration of this man knowing the people would spread the word quickly of the miracle that occurred.

Never Lose Hope

Scripture reveals the demon-possessed man was now fully clothed (which indicates he previously was not and adds to the bizarre character of this story). This man had been uncontrollable. Lonely. Confused. Hurting himself and hurting others. Occasionally lucid only to plunge under again. Now he was sitting with Jesus, healed and completely restored.

But the people who had witnessed this miracle responded in an unexpected way:

> Then those who had seen what happened told the others about the demon-possessed man and the pigs. And the crowd began pleading with Jesus to go away and leave them alone. As Jesus was getting into the boat, the man who had been demon possessed begged to go with him. But Jesus said, "No, go home to your family, and tell them everything the Lord has done for you and how merciful he has been." — **Mark 5:16–19 (NLT)**

There will always be some who experience the power and presence of God in a real way and won't be able to handle it. Some in the crowd begged Jesus to "go away and leave them alone" (Mark 5:17). Jesus listened to them and left. He didn't force Himself on them—but man, did they miss out.

I find that we are no different than the people in our churches today. If the Holy Spirit shows up, if Jesus really ushers in a miracle, if something supernatural happens, many people become uncomfortable.

Because of this, I have started to make this my prayer, and maybe you can, too: *God, I have enough natural— give me supernatural. God, I am used to the ordinary— give me extraordinary.*

The next verses are my favorite part of the story. It's the beautiful mention of the man's family. Can you imagine being his mother? His brother? His wife? His friend?

Some of you *do* know what this is like. You have had a front row seat to someone else's canvas of pain. Imagine what it was like for this family to know their son or brother was living in the place of the dead. Perhaps they were forced to make the choice to send him there to the graveyard under pressure from the community. Can you imagine their intense feelings of guilt? They had given up on him. They had failed him. He was in a place he would never come back from, and they knew it.

But then they heard some chatter—they heard people marveling, and their ears perked up because they realized their friend, their son, or their husband was the man these folks were talking about.

Then, just as they were trying to decide if they should go out to the graveyard to look for him, they saw him coming, and they ran as fast as they could to meet him. He was clean and sober. He was making wise choices. He had met Jesus. The one who was dead to them was now alive!

The lesson to learn from the story of the demon-possessed man is *never to lose hope.* Maybe there is someone in your life who has made you think, "It's too late." They have been addicted too long. Their mental illness is too much. They haven't sought God in years. They are making unwise choices. They don't love you anymore—the relationship is over.

Never lose hope! One day you may see them walk toward you fully clothed in God's righteousness and healed.

When a person is healed by the power of the resurrected Jesus, they cannot keep silent. The demon-possessed man had a message to share with anyone who would listen. He journeyed to the "Ten Towns of that region and began to proclaim the great things Jesus had done for him; and everyone was amazed at what he told them" (Mark 5:20 NLT). I would love to own a t-shirt from that tour!

The man obeyed what Jesus told him to do with his life. When God changes a person—when they fully grasp the freedom and power of the gospel and what great things He has done for them—they stop worrying about what others did to them. Or for those who have been successful, they stop thinking that their life is their own making.

Perhaps you have a "benign" story—no demons, no chains. Do you recognize your story is one of God saving you from heartache because you obeyed Him—or even if you didn't? Except for His grace, you could even now be the man in the dead place.

You have a story to tell, of one kind or another. This transformed man wanted to tell the world!

What's your story? Who is hearing it? Whom can you encourage and believe God's best for, by never giving up on them?

Your pain has become your professor. Pain can begin to define your purpose and ultimately lead others to your Savior.

Chapter 6 Questions

Question: What is a source of pain you're experiencing or have experienced in your life? How have you related or connected to God in your pain? How can you express your hope and thankfulness amidst suffering?

_____

_____

_____

_____

_____

_____

_____

_____

_____

_____

Question: What external enemies or obstacles are you confronting in your life right now? What internal enemies are you facing? Name them!

_____

_____

_____

_____

_____

_____

_____

_____

_____

_____

_____

_____

Question: What is your story? Who are you telling? How can you do more to encourage others in the Lord with your story of transformation through pain?

_____

_____

_____

_____

_____

_____

_____

_____

_____

_____

Action: When your pain seems overwhelming, look to the One in charge! Take the time to name your enemies and identify the obstacles you're facing—especially those in your own heart. Meanwhile, never lose hope that God will help you endure and overcome. Then encourage others with the story of how He sustained you in your suffering and gave your pain a purpose!

Chapter 6 Notes

_____

_____

_____

_____

_____

_____

_____

_____

_____

_____

_____

_____

_____

_____

_____

_____

_____

_____

_____

_____

_____

_____

_____

_____

CHAPTER SEVEN

When God Moves

Sometimes the places Jesus takes people are far more about the journey than the destination. What you are going through may not be about where God is *taking* you, but about what He is *teaching* you.

After the miraculous healing of the demon-possessed man, Jesus continued to teach His disciples. Scripture says He "got into the boat again and went back to the other side of the lake, where a large crowd gathered around him on the shore" (Mark 5:21 NLT).

Another great story of hope was about to take place. Remember, this whole account started when Jesus decided to take the disciples across the lake the first time (Mark 4:35). In retrospect, we can see that the real reason Jesus made that trip was to teach His disciples. But geographically, they were now right back where they started.

Coming from Behind

Not surprisingly, word about Jesus had spread. The man in the Gerasenes graveyard whom everyone had written off had become a beacon of hope, and people were paying attention—including a man named Jairus:

> Then a leader of the local synagogue, whose name was Jairus, arrived. When he saw Jesus, he fell at his feet, pleading fervently with him. "My little daughter is dying," he said. "Please come and lay your hands on her; heal her so she can live." — **Mark 5:22–23 (NLT)**

Jairus, a religious leader with a dying daughter, had heard the chatter. Notice Jairus's posture upon seeing Jesus—he fell at His feet. Falling at Jesus' feet is a symbol of worship and of surrender. It is a stance that is ready to receive.

Jesus responded by going with Jairus, but His journey was quickly interrupted:

> Jesus went with him, and all the people followed, crowding around him. A woman in the crowd had suffered for twelve years with constant bleeding. She had suffered a great deal from many doctors, and over the years she had spent everything she had to pay them, but she had gotten no better. In fact, she had gotten worse. — **Mark 5:24–26 (NLT)**

Once again, Jesus gathered a crowd. A large crowd. People were pushing in and walking beside Him, fighting for the best view, anxious to see what was going to happen next. The woman had suffered for twelve years with continual bleeding and was considered unclean by Jewish law. She could not be touched or touch anyone. She could not worship at the temple. She was a social outcast.

> She had heard about Jesus. So she came up behind him through the crowd and touched his robe. For she thought to herself, "If I can just touch his robe, I will be healed." — **Mark 5:27–28 (NLT)**

Note the woman's posture: she came from behind. Have you ever been in a season where you felt like you were coming from behind? Always in survival mode. Trying to catch up in life.

Did you know, this is not what God intends for you? The Bible says that the people of God will be made the head, not the tail (Deuteronomy 28:13). They are above, not below. They are God's church, the bride of Christ.

We are not behind—we are in the front of what God is doing.

Literally and figuratively, the bleeding woman was at her lowest. How would she even know which one was Jesus?

In first-century Jewish culture, the hem of Jesus' robe would have had a marking of identity. It is striking to me that even when she was crawling on the ground, Jesus made it possible to find Him. His name was on His robe—and there is power in the name of Jesus. When the woman reached out in faith and touched it, a miracle occurred:

> Immediately the bleeding stopped, and she could feel in her body that she had been healed of her terrible condition. Jesus realized at once that healing power

had gone out from him, so he turned around in the crowd and asked, "Who touched my robe?" His disciples said to him, "Look at this crowd pressing around you. How can you ask, 'Who touched me?'" But he kept on looking around to see who had done it. Then the frightened woman, trembling at the realization of what had happened to her, came and fell to her knees in front of him and told him what she had done. And he said to her, "Daughter, your faith has made you well. Go in peace. Your suffering is over." — **Mark 5:29–34 (NLT)**

The exterior of a person who has been healed doesn't always change immediately, but the woman felt the inner change instantly. Everyone was bumping into Jesus. Everyone was reaching for God, but only one *touched* Him. Only one in that crowd had the expectation that touching Jesus would change everything—it was the woman's faith that made her well (Mark 5:34 NLT). Expectancy is the precursor to a miracle of God!

God will meet you at the level of your expectation. The bleeding woman believed healing would come from a mere touch—and indeed, her faith made her well.

After she had been healed, consider how the woman's posture changed—she now knelt *in front* of Jesus. She was no longer behind. What happened inside of her was working its way out. Now she could look Him in the eyes. Now she could worship. And Jesus gave her a beautiful proclamation: "Your suffering is over" (Mark 5:34 NLT).

She was a nobody who decided to be a somebody. Her action of faith declared, "I am going to be a someone! I am going to be healed by this man." Her expectancy brought her into a new position, that of "daughter," and it gave her a new purpose for her life. She had become a child of God because of her faith (Galatians 3:26).

For children of the King, suffering is over. Their position in Christ overrides all pain.

Listen to Jesus, Not the Crowd

Recall that Jesus was on His way to Jairus's home when the miracle with the woman occurred. While Jesus was still speaking to her, Jairus received news about his daughter's condition from some messengers:

> They told him, "Your daughter is dead. There's no use troubling the Teacher now." But Jesus overheard them and said to Jairus, "Don't be afraid. Just have faith." — **Mark 5:35–36 (NLT)**

There will always be people who will rain doubt on your destiny. Had Jairus listened to the messengers or the crowd, he may have missed the miracle. Don't listen to what others say about Jesus. Listen to Him!

Jairus asked for help for his daughter—but Jesus knew Jairus's faith needed to be stronger. So Jesus allowed for this miracle of healing the woman in the crowd, as a sort of parenthetical statement to clarify and drive home the message Jairus needed to understand. Jairus heard Jesus proclaim she was well because of her faith, revealing that he too didn't need to listen to the natural or the ordinary—the cry of the crowd.

So, too, must we live today. The "cries of the crowd" will tell you Jesus has no power to do anything, and that faith in Him is a fairytale. Like Jairus, cling to the miracles you have already heard or personally experienced.

What Do You Expect?

We end this book with a miracle being ushered in through expectation. Jairus expected a miracle. His faith propelled him to bring Jesus to his home. Some in the crowd, however, did not believe:

> Then Jesus stopped the crowd and wouldn't let anyone go with him except Peter, James, and John (the brother of James). When they came to the home of the synagogue leader, Jesus saw much commotion and weeping and wailing. He went inside and asked, "Why all this commotion and weeping? The child isn't dead; she's only asleep."
>
> The crowd laughed at him. But he made them all leave, and he took the girl's father and mother and his three disciples into the room where the girl was lying. Holding her hand, he said to her, "Talitha koum," which means "Little girl, get up!" And the girl, who was twelve years old, immediately stood up and walked around! They were overwhelmed and totally amazed.
> — **Mark 5:37–42 (NLT)**

Jesus stopped the first crowd from coming. They were pushing in around Him, but they did not have faith that a miracle could happen. They were just observers. How many other people in that multitude needed help from Jesus? Yet the woman who touched His robe was the only one whose faith brought about a miracle.

Jesus sent the second crowd away. When it was time for another miracle, Jesus chose three expectant disciples—Peter, James, and John—and the dead girl's father and mother, as witnesses.

The crowds and even the other disciples would only see the result of the miracle. But Jesus allowed a few faith-filled men and women to be in the front row.

Do you expect God to answer prayers?

Do you expect to see change in your life and in others' lives?

Do you have faith that will reach out and touch the hem of Jesus' garment—knowing He will heal?

Do you expect a movement of God when you join in fellowship with other believers? Or are you like the believers in Acts 12 who, when the answer to their prayer knocked on the door, didn't believe? Are you praying like a practical atheist?

Your expectancy is your ticket to see the extraordinary. Expect Jesus for the miracle you need in your life.

He will show up!

Chapter 7 Questions

Question: What influences in your life are trying to undermine your faith? How can you resist these influences in a Jesus-like way?

_____

_____

_____

_____

_____

_____

_____

_____

_____

_____

_____

Question: In what areas of life are you currently seeking God for help? How completely do you trust Him for a miracle? How should your trust be demonstrated?

_____

_____

_____

_____

_____

_____

_____

_____

_____

_____

_____

Question: How has God moved in your life in response to prayer? With whom can you join in prayer regularly?

_____

_____

_____

_____

_____

_____

_____

_____

_____

_____

Action: Don't let other people or the culture around you undermine your faith! Instead, seek God in prayer daily and in all things, and expect Him to answer. Join with others in prayer, too, and believe God will work healing and other miracles in response—even if His miracle isn't exactly what you expected. Trust Him to move in your life as you earnestly seek Him!

Chapter 7 Notes

CONCLUSION

Don't Miss the Miracles

This book has uncovered seven distinct miracles of Jesus. His personal care was evident in a situation as "unimportant" as running out of wine at a wedding, as well as in a situation involving a grieving father whose child had died.

A miracle isn't a magic trick; it requires the investment of complete obedience. Jesus worked in different ways and used various means to accomplish His plan— always to increase people's faith.

What may not make sense now in your life could, in fact, be the beginning of a miracle. However, it is faith that will stir the miracle to fruition. Trust God to bring forth a miracle in your life like the Shunammite woman dreamt of a son. Trust Him with enough faith, as Mary did, that He *can* perform a miracle—even if you know He might not. Trust Jesus even if He has said "no" to your cries, like the man with the sick son who was sent home.

Like the blind man at the pool of Bethesda, stand up and get off your mat when Jesus commands you to move. Leave past fears, insecurities, and other concerns behind.

Trust Him during the storms of your life—His presence is with you, and that is all you need. Claim who you are in Christ, ready to be set free and to become whom God made you to be, like the bleeding woman. Chase down a miracle as Jairus did, and believe tenaciously, even after you're told it's too late.

And finally, strive to be like Peter, James, and John—some of the privileged few with a track record of faith who caught the eye of the Savior. They were invited to be a part of the extraordinary things God was doing in changing others' lives.

Don't miss the miracles happening every day around you as people's hearts are moved toward God. We have a saying at Freedom Church that I think should become a mantra for you as well:

We are not praying for a miracle of God, We ARE a miracle of God.

Perhaps a miracle is being birthed at this moment—in you.

Notes

1. "Miracle." *Merriam-Webster.* https://www.merriam-webster.com/dictionary/miracle

2. "Miracles." *Christian Answers. Network.* https://www.christiananswers.net/dictionary/miracle.html

3. Morris, Leon. *The Gospel According to John.* Wm. B. Eerdmans Publishing Co., 1971, pp. 178–179.

4. Peterson, Eugene H. *A Long Obedience in the Same Direction: Discipleship in an Instant Society.* InterVarsity Press, 2000.

5. "Strong's G5199 – hygiēs." *Blue Letter Bible.* https://www.blueletterbible.org/lang/lexicon/lexicon.cfm?t=niv&strongs=g5199

6. Lewis, C. S. *The Four Loves.* Mariner Books, 1971.

7. "Matthew 14:25." *Bible Hub*. http://biblehub.com/commentaries/matthew/14-25.htm

8. "Full Text of 'The Narragansett Order.'" Archive. https://archive.org/stream/narragansetthistv7rhod/narragansetthistv7rhod_djvu.txt

9. Whitbourne, Susan Krauss. "5 Reasons We Play the Blame Game But Rarely Win." *Psychology Today*. 19 September 2015. https://www.psychologytoday.com/blog/fulfillment-any-age/201509/5-reasons-we-play-the-blame-game

10. "What Is the Glory of God?" *Got Questions Ministries*. https://www.gotquestions.org/glory-of-God.html

11. Ibid.

12. Nine Inch Nails. "Hurt." Lyrics by Trent Reznor. *Downward Spiral*. Nothing Records/Interscope Records, 1994.

About the Author

Pastor Shawn grew up in Moncks Corner, SC, and graduated from Berkeley High School. Shawn Wood is the Lead Pastor and Founding Pastor of Freedom Church in Moncks Corner. Previously, Shawn was the Experiences and Creative Communications Pastor and a Teaching Pastor at Seacoast Church in Mount Pleasant, SC.

He is the author of *200 Pomegranates and an Audience of One*, *Wasabi Gospel*, and *In the Stillness*. Shawn and his wife Connie have four children: Isabelle, Hayes, Sam, and Nia.

Shawn loves Connie and their kids. He really likes the Gamecocks and the Patriots, and he has a love–hate relationship with Krispy Kreme Donuts that he would rather not discuss.

Thank you to my editors at Sermon To Book for helping
to make this book happen.